SKID STEERS

Mark and Christina Sinclair

To our little skids steers,
Tovi and Connor,
who are changing everyday.
~Mommy and Daddy

Copyright © 2018 by Christina A. Sinclair and Mark A. Sinclair
All rights reserved. This book or any portion thereof may not be reproduced or used in any manner whatsoever without the express written permission of the publisher except for the use of brief quotations in a book review.

ISBN-13: 978-1729792742
ISBN-10: 172979274X

Photo Credits

Attribution ShareAlike 3.0 Unported, https://creativecommons.org/licenses/by-sa/3.0, from Wikimedia Commons:
Title Page & Page 13: By Zralok1, https://commons.wikimedia.org/wiki/File:Smykem_%C5%99%C3%ADzen%C3%BD_naklada%C4%8D_GEHL_5240_v_ter%C3%A9nu.jpg#filelinks.
Page 9 Middle: By Luis Miguel Bugallo Sánchez, https://commons.wikimedia.org/wiki/File:Escavadora_003.jpg
Page 15 Bottom Left: By Adamantios, https://commons.wikimedia.org/wiki/File:Bobcat-S300-with-wheel-saw-attachment-0a.jpg
Page 15 Top Right: By Stehr-Baumaschinen, https://commons.wikimedia.org/wiki/File:Bobcat_T_300.jpg
Page 15 Bottom Right: By ~riley, https://commons.wikimedia.org/wiki/File:Bobcat_T190.JPG
Page 17: By Zralok1, https://commons.wikimedia.org/wiki/File:Smykem_%C5%99%C3%ADzen%C3%BD_naklada%C4%8D_Gehl_V270_vertik%C3%A1ln%C3%AD_zdvih.jpg
Page 23 Top Left: By Tennen-Gas, https://commons.wikimedia.org/wiki/File:Bobcat_001.JPG
Page 23 Bottom Middle: By Norbert Schnitzler, https://commons.wikimedia.org/wiki/File:Gehl_1640_vl.jpg

Attribution Generic 2.0, https://creativecommons.org/licenses/by/2.0), from Wikimedia Commons:
Page 6: By Metropolitan Transportation Authority of the State of New York (Weekend work 2012-07-09 04Uploaded by tm), https://commons.wikimedia.org/wiki/File:Weekend_work_2012-07-09_04_(7535301802).jpg
Page 9 Top Right: By Elisha Dawkins via Official Navy Page from United States of America, https://commons.wikimedia.org/wiki/File:Seabees_deployed_to_Guantanamo_Bay_take_part_in_construction_project..jpg
Page 13 Bottom Left: Master Sgt. Denice Rankin, https://www.flickr.com/photos/bcmichguard/13986595436/.
Page 16: Photo by Tina Shaw/USFWS, https://www.flickr.com/photos/usfwsmidwest/7162909115/.
Page 23 Bottom Left: https://www.flickr.com/photos/adeleprince/9930745933/.

Attribution ShareAlike 2.0 Generic, https://creativecommons.org/licenses/by-sa/2.0/, from Wikimedia Commons:
Page 10: By USA Attachments https://www.flickr.com/photos/30568962@N07/2869410138/.
Page 13 Top Right: USA Attachments, https://www.flickr.com/photos/30568962@N07/2868585095/.
Page 14: By Greg Goebel from Loveland CO, USA, https://commons.wikimedia.org/wiki/File:Caterpillar_246C_with_brush_cutter.jpg

Cover: M.ribac31 [CC BY-SA 4.0 (https://creativecommons.org/licenses/by-sa/4.0)], from Wikimedia Commons. https://commons.wikimedia.org/wiki/File:1650R.jpg
Page 5: U.S. Navy photo by Mass Communication Specialist 2nd Class Nathan Laird [Public domain], via Wikimedia Commons, https://commons.wikimedia.org/wiki/File:US_Navy_101116-N-7241L-008_Builder_3rd_Class_Ace_Shedd,_assigned_to_Naval_Mobile_Construction_Battalion_(NMCB)_7,.jpg
Page 7, 12, 15 (Middle Right), 18-20, 26: Clark Equipment Company
Page 8: FEMA/Robert Kaufmann, https://commons.wikimedia.org/wiki/File:FEMA_-_38755_-_Loader_operator_clears_a_street_of_debris_in_Texas.jpg
Page 9 Bottom Left: Photo: Cpl Russ Nolan RLC/MOD, https://commons.wikimedia.org/wiki/File:Armoured_CAT_Forklift_Truck_MOD_45149017.jpg
 [OGL (http://www.nationalarchives.gov.uk/doc/open-government-licence/version/1/)], via Wikimedia Commons
Page 9 Bottom Right: Photo: MC1 Carmichael Yepez, https://commons.wikimedia.org/wiki/File:US_Navy_070125-N-0775Y-051_Equipment_Operator_Constructionman_Albert_Amozarrutia,_a_Seabee_assigned_to_Naval_Mobile_Construction_Battalion_Three_(NMCB-3)_operates_a_rotary_brush_during_a_runway_repair_exercise_at_Kadena_Air_Bas.jpg
Page 13 Top Left: By Ildar Sagdejev (Specious), https://commons.wikimedia.org/wiki/File:2009-02-23_Skid_steer_with_extreme_duty_auger.jpg
 CC BY-SA 4.0 (https://creativecommons.org/licenses/by-sa/4.0), from Wikimedia Commons
Page 23 Top Right: By Redline, https://commons.wikimedia.org/wiki/File:Amkodor_03.JPG
 [GFDL (http://www.gnu.org/copyleft/fdl.html), CC BY-SA 2.5 (https://creativecommons.org/licenses/by-sa/2.5)], from Wikimedia Commons
99yllllllll]pp

TABLE OF CONTENTS

What is a Skid Steer?   4
Why Do We Need Skid Steers?   6
What Are the Parts of a Skid Steer?   10
Other Skid Steers   22
Glossary   24
Index   25

What is a Skid Steer?

A skid steer is a **compact** machine that can do many different jobs. The machine has fixed wheels or tracks, which means the wheels cannot turn side to side. The skid steer changes directions by varying the speed of the wheels on each side. When one side spins faster than the other, it makes the machine turn toward the slow side. When this happens, the wheels on the slower side skid across the ground, and that is where these amazing machines get their name.

Why Do We Need Skid Steers?

Skid steers are very useful because they can work and turn around in very tight spaces, such as underground railroads or backyards.

Skid steers are **versatile** because they can move dirt, rocks or **debris.** Skid steers can also drill, cut, dig, lift, sweep and clean.

debris

What Are the Parts of a Skid Steer?

Skid steers have tires or tracks that can **maneuver** on different types of surfaces. However, their wheels do not turn like a car, they are always straight.

track

Skid steers can use many different tools that attach to the lift arm. These tools are called **attachments**, which can be used for different jobs. The most common attachments include buckets for heavy loads, forks for pallet moving, blades to push dirt or rock, brooms to clean, drills for digging holes, and jack hammers for demolition.

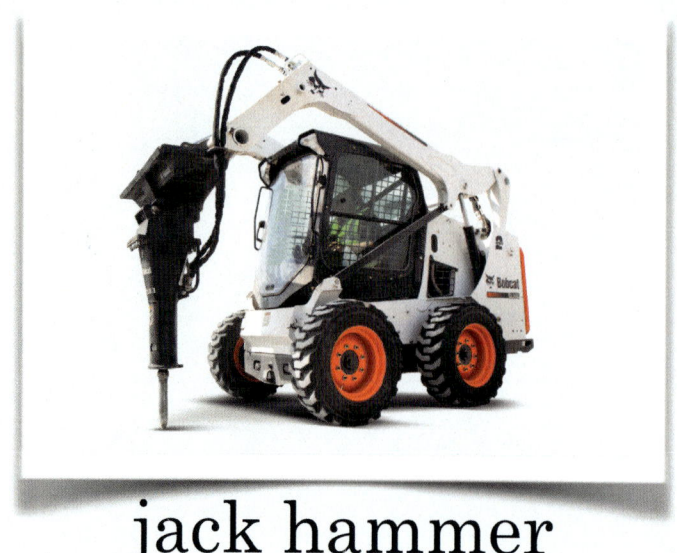

jack hammer

drill attachment

fork attachment

sweeper attachment

bucket attachment

There are also some less common attachments like brush cutters, snow blowers, wheel saws to cut through concrete, power box rakes to till the soil, plate compactors to compress soil and gravel, and trenchers to dig trenches for pipes or electrical cables.

brush cutter

Most skid steers have lift arms that run alongside both sides of the driver. The arms lift and lower the attachments by using **hydraulic** pumps. The lift arms attach in the back to keep the machine compact.

Skid steer drivers or operators sit inside the **cab**. To get into most skid steers, they step onto the attachment and crawl through the front. The operator controls the skid steer and the attachments with foot pedals and joysticks. The joysticks have buttons and switches for more control options.

Some skid steers have side screens to protect the operator from moving objects outside the cab. Some cabs protect the operator if the machine rolls over or if something falls on the cab. This is called the rollover protection system, or ROPS.

Other Skid Steers

Skid steers are amazing machines. They come in a variety of shapes and sizes. How many buckets can you find?

Glossary

attachment - a special tool that can be added to a machine or piece of equipment to make it able to do a particular job

compact - closely and neatly packed together

cab - the part of the skid steer where the driver sits

debris - pieces of waste or remains of something that was destroyed

hydraulics - using pressurized fluid to move an attached part, such as the lift arms

maneuver - a movement requiring skill and care

versatile - having many uses or the ability to adapt to different situations

Index

attachment, 12-14, 16, 18, 24
cab, 18, 20, 24
compact, 4, 16, 24
debris, 8, 24
driver, 16, 18
hydraulics, 16, 24
joystick, 18-19
lift arm, 12, 16-17
maneuver, 10, 24
operator, 18, 20
ROPS, 20-21
versatile, 8, 24

Special thanks to
Joe Leonard, Joan Leonard,
and
Clark Equipment Company,
https://www.bobcat.com/

Made in the USA
Columbia, SC
13 September 2019